Dear No one,

Coreanna Hunter

BookLeaf Publishing
India | USA | UK

Presentation by *BookLeaf Publishing*

Web: www.bookleafpub.com

E-mail: info@bookleafpub.com

ISBN: 9789357445672

First edition 2022

DEDICATION

To anyone to feel the way I did and sometimes still do. We are all amazing!

ACKNOWLEDGEMENT

I would like to thank my high school English and history teachers for one teaching me things I'll always use in my personal life as well as letting me read in classes they were my favorites. A special thanks to the people in my life that helped inspire these poems. And to Patricia Brucki my high school librarian, cross country coach, poetry club leader and second mother. I would not have made it out of high school without her.

PREFACE

All of these poems were written from the heart
and should be read that way as well. I want you
feel what it was I felt at the time.

Double Resurrection

Whenever we're together no matter how dark
the world around us is my universe is full of
spark
You say I led you out of the dark and brought
you into the light
But did you ever wonder how I got there?
I had fallen victim to my own demons
They were dragging me to my absolute breaking
point
And on the way down I found you- drowning in
your own demons and sorrows
Still to this day I don't know what it was but
something in me needed to be near you
The closer we got, the more I understood why.
My time with you feels better than a relaxation
sigh
Actually seeing you makes me so happy people
ask me am I high
The literal answer is no
The technical answer is yes
I'm high on the feeling of being with someone
and not having to hide from them
You've stripped away your amor to let me into
your soul

By doing so you gently chipped away at the
barriers I built to protect myself from everything
and everyone.
Ever since I was little I was told everyone had a
someone
Oh, how I thank God that you're mine
I took you coming into my life as a sign, a sign
that life isn't all for not.
And you're my shot, my shot at true happiness
and peace
You make the monsters in my head cease and
desist their assault on my stability
You make me believe I can beat any enemy
against me no matter their level of ability
You are definitely the greatest blessing God has
given me and the funny part is I wasn't looking
for you when we met,
But you turned out to be everything I was
looking for and then some

The Eternal Dance

I want to dance with you under the moon light
and star lit sky
Soft music playing at the rhythm of our beating
hearts
I want it to be a never ending tango
Please don't ever let go
If ever feeling uncertain just pull me closer
Small moments spent with you are worth more
than gold
We can laugh until we're old
You have always been bold
There was nothing you could be told
Until I came into the fold
Both forever changed
Sadly estranged
But that could change
I know we have the range
Ambitions run high
Especially on a runners high
You take me so high
You know I can not lie
I see you and I breathe a deep sigh
Full of relief
Not to my disbelief

Because you are a thief
The thief of my heart
In this dance may we never truly part again
I pray to God and say amen.

I'm Fine

Every now and then people ask me "are you
okay?"
Usually I lie and say " I'm fine I'm just tired"
That's not a full lie
I am tired.....
of the anxiety
The depression
The constant anger and deafening thoughts
The nights I spend crying my eyes out because I
can't hold in my pain any longer
And I'm tired of pretending like I'm okay
Because I don't trust anyone enough to hold my
vulnerability in their hands and not miss treat it

At least once a day I have to either force a smile
or push through the mountains of dysfunctional
thoughts my mind has forced me to live with
Everyday I have to act like I'm not dying a
miserable and slow death

Then there are those beautiful days where I don't
have to pretend because for once I actually can
smile with my whole heart
But those never get to live long

They are always cut short
Giving me an even shorter leash to hang by
That's almost always when someone asks me my
favorite question
"Are you okay?"
There's only one thing I can say
"I'm fine"
All the while I'm thinking to myself
"My life hurts, why won't it just end already?"

I'm honest to a fault
You can ask me almost anything and is answer
honestly
But when it comes to my feelings my lips are
like a vault
Locked tight and I forgot the code
I don't want to lie to some
But I also don't need them to worry about me
I definitely don't need them looking at me
differently

It Doesn't Hurt You

Your words don't hurt you
They hurt those around you
Which is why you're never careful with them
Of course you'd be cautious if your own health
was at risk
But these brushes with death are always too
brisk

It's never you who is hurt
Or your heart that bleeds with the soreness of a
thousand mega hert bolts
You never feel the sting of your words
Which is why you use them like swords
Not caring who it hurts
Even the people you claim to love most bare the
burden of your cruelty to the fullest

Sharp words spiteful heart
When you're supposed to have kind words
loving heart
Projecting your inner self hate on to her
"Oh it's okay she can take it"

Well actually no she can't she's actually 3
seconds from trying to starve herself just to get
you to be quiet
Cuz maybe then She can get away from your
voice piercing through the layers of hardened
defenses she's built over the years to drown you
out
But now in her 17th year her armor is cracking
and falling off
She can't rebuild it fast enough to protect herself
from the persistent hurt your words afflict on her
But all you see is a lazy secretive, selfish girl

Venom

Projectile,
Volatile,
Gladiatorial
Fatal.
This is what describes venom.
Which is what you are to me,
You force your way into my body, and
I can feel you burning through me from the
inside out as you slither your way through my
veins poisoning every single thing you touch.
My mind was the very first thing to be infected
by you and ever since then I haven't been the
same
You set my sensibility a flame- it's burning blaze
refuses to die down enough to let me breathe
through the smoke
Everyday I think I might choke and you just
think it's a joke
You make me seem irrational
And overly emotional
But to me I truly am near my end
To everyone else it looks like my reality was
made to bend - bend outta shape into a
complicated maze

That even I its creator can not make it out of
You have poisoned my thoughts over and over
each dose more deadly than the last
Each breathe so frantic I don't know why I
haven't taken my last
I didn't know my heart could beat this fast
People always say "it's okay just calm down"
"it's not a big deal you need to chill"
Oh trust me if I could I would

The Helper

To be helpful,
To assist in every way,
To make your peace plentiful,
To make your dark lingering shadows go away.

These are the things I have set my purpose in
life to be.
To set your soul free while it still inhabits your
body.
You have never put this responsibility on me,
So please know what this means to me.

When I feel the pain of your heart traveled over
distance it tortures me that much worse.
My health is intertwined with yours and the
bond may never be undone.
It is my only one,
The only one that makes me care,
And when something is wrong, I am faced with
despair.

My soul's desire is to be helpful,
To assist in every way.
To make your peace plentiful,

To make your dark lingering shadows go away.
        But I have failed more than once,
I have used all of my energy; every ounce.
A normal person whom hasn't felt the magic of
your presence would stop.
Thank God I don't know how.
Even with my failed attempts please allow me to
be your helper.

Trust

Trust is like a mirror
Once it is broken you can put the pieces back
together to see yourself again
But not without the cracks left behind
No matter how well you put the mirror back
together it's still has the cracks
But that doesn't mean you can't do it well
enough to see your reflection clearly
Just takes an enormous amount of time,
patience, and effort

Trust
Trust me when I say I never trusted anyone more
With my thoughts
With my feelings
With my doubts and insecurities
With me
I trusted you with everything I had and I did it
blindly
So blindly I couldn't see what was coming
I couldn't see your fear
And fear is dangerous
Fear makes some of the best people make some
of the worst decisions

Trust
Trust that I still love you with everything I am
That I still think about you when I wake up and
right before I go to sleep
That I say a prayer for you every now and again
That you still run through my mind when I listen
to music
That I still remember your favorite things

Trust
Trust that I want to be with you
But know that I don't trust you
It's not that I don't want to
I'm just afraid to
Trust that I love you
I never want to be afraid of what you might do
So please show me something new

Turn the Page

Turn, turn, turn the page
Read the words
Feel what they mean to you
Let yourself travel as far as you want to
Every new page is a new beginning
Every new word is a new feeling

Turn, turn, turn the page
Put yourself in new shoes
Give yourself new point of views
Let yourself think in new ways
Free yourself from your mental disarray's

Turn, turn, turn the page
Let yourself drift off
Allow the words to sweep you off your feet
Float for as long as you want

Turn, turn, turn the page
Release your thoughts from their shackles
Let your imagination run free

Turn, turn, turn the page

Funny Faces

Funny faces
Funny faces
All I see are funny faces
Different races
Different paces
Different places
All of these different faces
Most wear masks
Some wear full costumes
Few are real
Most hide behind a shield
Some hide behind a lie
Few brave enough to ride the wave of
uncertainty that is other people
Their faces
All their funny faces
All their paces and races
All these different places
It gets overwhelming
It's overbearing
It's too much
All these funny faces
Different places
Funny cases

Different paces run together
It wouldn't be too bad if more people were brave
enough for the truth
See, the truth is difficult but not scary
All these funny faces I can't tell which ones are
real
And which ones are fake
I hate these funny face.

Where am I

Where am I today?
Am I in the past?
Reliving all my past mistakes?
Going over old conversations like I could change them now?
Analyzing my most upsetting memories while simultaneously running from them?
Regretting the thoughts and feelings I've shared with people?
Doubting every decision I've made leading to this point?
Or, am I in the future?
In a future that does not exist?
Am I making plans as if God hasn't shown me my path already?
Am I in my head but not really there?
Zoned out, checked out wishing I was knocked out?
Never paying attention to the here and now, making me miss it every now and again.
Where am I today?
Have I found that middle ground?
Have I figured out how to plan for the future while keeping my heart and mind open?

Have I figured out how to reminisce without
getting stuck in the rut of my past?
Have I finally figured out how to live inside
AND outside?
Have I found the here and now?
Since I'm still asking I'll say no I haven't quite
found it yet.
I'm missing some direction yet,
Can't seem to find the good maps.
I refuse to fall through the gaps.
At my lowest I almost snapped,
It would've been a cap.
Yeah, no cap.
But don't worry Cap,
I'm finding my way.
I'm on my way,
That's all I can say.

Love Vs Fear

What's love got to do with it?
Everything.
Everything is governed between love and fear
If you operate in fear it breeds destruction and
confusion
If you operate in love it creates abundance and
clarity
The energy we hold is just as important as the
energy we share if not more so
What you keep around you can determine your
success or failure
Fill your environment with your soul's rightful
nourishment and you flourish
Fill your environment with poison and the soul
begins to die just as a tree would with poisoned
soil
Fear is weak and brisk
It'll break you and everything around it in an
instant
Fear is controlling and suffocating
It'll push you into a corner and take your breathe
away until you stop fighting to get free
This is always
Love is strong and everlasting

Once you love someone or something you never
stop
This allows you to grow and expand as needed
even away from what and whom no longer
serves you
Love is freeing and flowing
It will let you fly as you need to in order to let
you be you
This is always
To love and to be loved would not put you in
chains
It'll make you dance outside when it rains
To fear and to be fearful of love will cause you
to cry more than the sky in a thunderstorm

Manifested Love

Is it just me or does the sun shine brighter when
you're happier?
At first I didn't know you were the one
In fact, I didn't want you to be
See I knew from the start of my aching heart
Loving you as I do
Would be the end of me
I'd do anything to see you smile
All the while
Your love and affections for me grew intensely
With each passing second and every sending
message my heart slowly stops beating for me
And begins to beat for you instead
All day you run through my head like a
marathon on repeat never missing a beat,
Every step you take in sync with my hearts
rhythmic tone
Letting me know I'm no longer alone
The bad part is
I get caught up in my perfect fantasies that the
breaking news of my reality slips away
That is until it's done being ignored

And trust me it never has a shy hello but instead
it does a loud bellow like a hungry beast
attacking it's prey
Oh how I pray for my fantasies to one day be
real
But it's not enough for it to be my souls desire it
must be yours as-well
I tend to excel in getting what I want in
whatever form I can get it and with you that
continues to be true but also false
Hopefully one day I will have to change that
statement
In knowing you I've grown a lot in every way
and so has the truth that you may be the death of
me and I'm okay with that

A Perfect Match

I'm in love with a girl I call Bonita
And I fall harder every time I look up into the
sky- uh
I don't know what to do with this
Its reach is further than the deepest arches of my
spirit
There's no easy way of explaining it
I know this isn't the end of it
What's needed?
A situation with mutual benefit
That's it
For the hell of it
For the love of it
She's my perfect fit
We make the perfect puzzle pieces
Two half's of one whole
Two hearts formed from one soul
Both the bad and the good meeting to make what
is meant to be
Each having both inside but not knowing how to
let them out
How to let their true selves breathe
To breathe in acceptance

And to breathe out the clouds of doubts that
plague our minds
To be who we are just as we are
The goofy dork that loves art, music, passion
and anime but is conventionally attractive so is
forced into boxes that actually don't explain who
she is
And she'd rather put up the facade that what
they think is really true rather than face rejection
 I can't say I blame her
And the quiet bookworm that feels cursed with
loneliness due to never fitting anyone's
expectations
And knows she never will
Due to this she doesn't know how to let others
see the parts of her that really matter
The essence of us melds together perfectly
But the amor we wear to protect ourselves
always clash and make us uncomfortable
I know what we need
To be vulnerable
To let our inner lights shine even if it's only to
each other
We could be a perfect match

Black Woman Queerness

To be a black woman. What does it mean to call oneself a black woman? There are tons of different stereotypes to choose from to describe black women and almost none of them are actually true. Majority if not all of them come from an expectation of who we are, what we like, how we speak, who we choose to love, how we look and think. All made from people and groups that do not understand what it is like to be us. Some of us are tall some, short. Some educated by books and schooling others, from life. Some are physically strong while others are internally powerful. Some prefer or feel more comfortable expressing themselves in the "normal" socially accepted feminine ways, and there are plenty that choose to express themselves purely through their own beliefs and feelings on what makes them feel like a woman, or not. And if one chooses to step out or is naturally born against what society accepts to be a black woman, a being society already does not accept; then they have just signed up to go to war for the rest of their lives. We have seen proof of this being true and we dare not be queer on top of that, we may as well call the national guard on ourselves. Because how dare a black woman be her own person, have her own dreams, thoughts, feelings, as-well as strength AND to love those that look like her. She's the most dangerous thing alive to be hated by most simply for existing and to still have the courage to be exactly who she was meant to be, love who she is and to love freely. She can not and will not be tamed which is exactly what those against her want, and they hate it but they can not stop it.

Star Crossed Lovers

My love for her feels like it's from another
dimension
It stretches from our real home all the way to
this destitute world we live in
And then stretches even further
Nothing makes me feel fuller
It's a never ending pinnacle of love
It's unconditional
It's uncontrollable
It's intensity can break through any barrier that
tries to keep us apart
Ever since our start
To me she is the most beautiful piece of art
In my life every moment with her is the best part
An interstellar love affair
Some are jealous and think it to be unfair
But we don't care
A love that's traveled light years to be
experienced refuses to be rejected
Can never be dejected
Doubt has been injected
But in our actions it can not be reflected
When I look into the night sky and see the North
Star I think of her

She's always been my way home
Don't know what to do
Or what to say
Or what's to come next
She's never a wrong answer
All my life I felt homesick even while at home
I knew home was something else
So much better
It was unexplainable
But I could never find it
Waited so long I wanted to give up
Until I met my star
Then home didn't feel too far

Chaos Grows, The Wicked Knows

They say the truly wicked run with chaos
They say only the wicked know the ins and outs
of destruction
They say savior is a long shot away for the
wicked
But these people don't know what the word
wicked is
The "wicked" are merely the ones scorned and
burned by society's rules and won't stand for it
They stand tall against it
Even when repeatedly knocked down and out
By the same rules that were supposed to help
and protect them
And they were only brought harm
The masses call them wicked
Only cause massa said so
It's sad they don't know
The master of the show
The one delivering every blow
The one making more chaos as the days go by

Watching bodies drop like a fly
Souls flying off into the sky
Families begging to know why
Oh me oh my
It's that guy
Taking our money to buy tanks
Taking our boys and instead of turning them to
men
He turns them into soldiers
Broken families
Broken dreams
Broken promises
Broken policies
The ones running with chaos are the ones
running the country

Time

Here on this swirling little rock we call home
time passes with no end
What a strange thing it is - time
Always going
Never ending
Never slows
Or accelerates
Yet as I speak to you as I always do, I realize
we've only been in each other's lives for some
months
But I was under the impression we'd been close
for all our lives

See from the logical standpoint I understand it's
merely been months
Months full of laughter, love, true happiness and
honesty no one can dare challenge
But with every passing second it feels like an
hour and every hour feels like a day every day
feels like a week
A week feels like a month and a month feels like
forever

Now I don't mean this in a boring drag kind of
way but in the way of saying,
I sometimes get so caught up in our time
together and how close we've grown to one
another
That I forget just how short our time has been
Then elation sets in because then I remember we
have so many more years and decades together
and they will be filled with a force stronger than
gravity and memories greater than time

Then I think again just how strange time is
And how the only thing that truly feels right is
my time with you

Potential

The first time you kiss me I want it to be
perfectly imperfect there is no perfect way for us
only what feels right
The first time you kiss me I want it to send me
to another world
Cause you're outta this world you're not like
everyone else
Nothing about you is basic
Some of your actions are a bit drastic
I know it's only because of the static
With you I'm never in a panic
When you came into my life everything got
swirled
And it whirled
Then sank but later soared
I don't have another way to say you're adored
Yes I do
This love of ours is not new
But feels fresher than the sweet morning due
So I send my words to make you swoon
To send your heart to the moon
I pray to see you soon.

Fragile Not Broken

Fragile not broken
I've always been fragile
But my fragility made way for me to become
broken
Scarred
Scared
Alone
I never wanted to be alone
I just got good at it
When you're by yourself the only one that can
hurt you is you
You know how far to go before it's too far
So you become your own bully
Better than all the movies you've seen
Even the battle scars you leave yourself last
longer than the bruises someone else can give
The best bullies are those who have been bullied
They know how to make it hurt
Make the pain of their words and punches linger
so you don't forget
Don't forget that this happens just cause you're
you
But it's worse when you're your own bully

When it's someone else it's easier to decide
enough is enough and fight back or tell someone
When it's you bullying yourself
That's almost impossible to admit
Even harder to stop
To turn around and fight yourself
Every thought
Every action
Every fear
Every insecurity
Is your own and you have to face every last one
of them
It's the hardest thing on Earth
But also the best thing
Once you start fighting you never stop
May take a break but you always get back up to
fight
Cause now you mean it
Cause now you're fighting for you life and you
refuse to lose
Even to yourself
Round after round
Bell after bell
You keep winning
You keep taking back the parts of you long lost
and forgotten
The best parts of you
Restored to it's original fragility

Only this time you know how to protect it
You don't hide it away
You never wanted that
But now you've found the groove of your fight
And your old self is bound to lose
But don't let up
Don't let em breathe
You take that breath away and use it to breathe
life into who you really are
Fill your lungs until you can't anymore
And let out the biggest sigh of relief you can
Your opponent has lost
You've fought and won back your life
Free to be as fragile as you are

Words

Words
We use them to communicate
Sometimes with loved ones
Sometimes with coworkers
Sometimes with total strangers
They can used with love and encouragement
Or they can be turned into swords
Words
Can have unlimited meaning
Or none at all
It all depends on how they're used and by who
they're used
A word from one person probably wouldn't even
register to you but the same word from another
could have the power to put you at the top of the
world or under the heaviest mountain
Words
Use them wisely
Speak what's most important
Don't just fill the air with words
You could be bringing on more than you planned
for
Speak on purpose with purpose
Say what you mean and mean what you say

The wrong or right word could make or break a
day
Words
"Sticks and stones may break my bones by
words will never hurt me"
Lies
Words have the power to heal as well as destroy
"Actions speak louder than words"
Not true
We just pay attention to actions more than words
but they hold the same volume
Sometimes all a person has are their words
So they are careful with who they share them
with
Words
Can be the beginning or the ending
But it's all depending
On if you use them as words or swords

Colors

I see colors everywhere
I see colors in everyone
I see colors in everything
I feel it in music
With every emotion
Every thought has its own color
And they swirl around to make beautiful shapes
and patterns
It's impossible to explain them all
To say I live like a kaleidoscope would be silly
But I'm a silly person
The color of a persons skin doesn't matter to me
Show me the color of your soul instead
It's a much better judge
The hippies had it right with the rainbow
collision
What happened to it
What happened to the colors of the world
Things have gotten bland
People have gotten bland
And it leaves a sour taste in my mouth
Someone please bring me some sugar

www.ingramcontent.com/pod-product-compliance
Lightning Source LLC
LaVergne TN
LVHW021306200726
843509LV00012B/1806